ACTIVITY BANK

Drugs

Terry Brown
and
Ian Harvey

Contents

Editor: Emma Ray
Layout artist: Suzanne Ward
Illustrations: Sarah Wimperis – Graham-Cameron Illustration

© 2000 Folens Limited, on behalf of the authors.

Every effort has been made to contact copyright holders of material used in this book. If any have been overlooked, we will be pleased to make any necessary arrangements.

First published 2000 by Folens Limited, Dunstable and Dublin.

Folens Limited, Albert House, Apex Business Centre, Boscombe Road, Dunstable, LU5 4RL, England.

ISBN 1 86202 562–2

Printed in Singapore by Craft Print.

How to use this book

There are 19 activities contained within this book. Each one has a teacher instruction page and a pupil activity page. The activities can be completed in short time slots or extended into longer periods, depending on the length of time you have available. They can also be differentiated to suit the needs of less able pupils. The activities can be presented in any order and you do not have to work your way right through the book. A matrix on page 56 provides a useful summary of, and reference to, the skills that pupils will learn through each activity, but we do recommend that Activity 1 and Activity 2 are presented as a starting point to your series of lessons and Activity 19 as a review at the end.

The Drug Files, Glossary and information about drug laws provide a useful resource for teachers to enhance the activities.

Most of the activities in this book need few materials or resources other than copies of the activity sheet, paper and pens. They are designed to keep the teacher's workload to a minimum beyond planning how each activity will be carried out in the classroom. Most are designed so that pupils can work individually, in pairs or in small groups, depending on the teacher's preference. We recommend a balance of whole class, small group and individual work to provide pupils with plenty of opportunity to express their views, to listen and to try to understand the views of others and to develop communication and social skills.

Teachers will also need to be aware of the sensitivities of the pupils' cultural and religious backgrounds when planning their lessons. If necessary, a letter could be sent to parents about the contents of the lessons in order to elicit their support.

The aims and expected outcomes of each activity are clearly indicated and the format for all activities is consistent to enable you quickly to feel comfortable and familiar with the style. All the information a teacher needs is contained here, not only to present the lesson confidently, but also to answer any questions that arise.

Introduction

Drug education is an important strand of the Government's ten-year strategy to tackle drug misuse, *Tackling Drugs to Build a Better Britain*.

The 1997 Ofsted report *Drug Education in Schools* suggests that 'schools should plan and provide a coherent and continuous drug education programme'.

The SCAA/DfEE publication *Drug Education: Curriculum Guidance for Schools* (SCAA/DfEE, 1995) suggests that 'the purpose of drug education should be to give young people the knowledge, skills and attitudes to appreciate the benefits of a healthy lifestyle and relate these to their own actions, both now and in their future lives.' It also offers an example outline drug education programme, detailing the knowledge and understanding, skills and attitudes that might be covered at each stage.

Protecting Young People: Good practice in drug education in schools and the youth service (DfEE, 1998) offers further guidance, including that 'drug education is most successfully delivered as part of a PSHE curriculum' and 'the most successful education programmes emphasise information and social skills ... as well as improvement in self-esteem and self-awareness and employ a range of teaching methods'.

The Framework for PSHE in the National Curriculum for the year 2000 includes drug education at each key stage.

Activity Bank: Drugs aims to support all of this guidance and offers an activity for each of the topics listed in the SCAA/DfEE example programme.

Encapsulating our needs

Pupil consultation

— AIMS —

To assess the pupils' needs in order to incorporate them as far as possible into future lessons.

Teaching Points

- The series of drug education lessons is flexible to allow it to be adapted to the level of knowledge and to the needs and concerns of the pupils.
- The activities are designed to be anonymous to encourage an open and honest response from the pupils, ensuring that as far as possible they meet their needs.
- Keep the sheet generated in Step 3 of this activity for use in Activity 19.
- Refer to the information gathered in this activity during the lessons that follow.

— USING THE ACTIVITY SHEET —

The focus of the activity is to draw out the thoughts and attitudes of the pupils before planning future lessons, in order to produce an effective series of lessons.

Step 1   Inform the pupils that this activity is intended to find out what they think is important in drug education so that their needs can be met. Hand out the activity sheets, to be completed as privately as possible.

Step 2   In small groups, prepare a composite response on a large enough piece of paper for display, to include a tally for items appearing more than once.

Step 3   Display all of the sheets and complete a class version, seeking clarification from pupils if necessary. Ask the pupils to decide on the importance of the items listed and inform them if there are any areas you cannot deal with. Otherwise, indicate that you will attempt to cover everything on this sheet in the lessons that follow and return to it at the end of the series of lessons to review progress.

Step 4   Ask the groups to discuss how the lesson was carried out and to feed back three words to describe it.

Extension Activities

- Using the activity sheet as a guide, ask pupils to design a questionnaire to ask their parents about their views on drug education. Compare the questionnaire with the opinions of the class.
- Ask the pupils to research one of the issues on the sheet and prepare a factsheet. Suggest that they use a library, the Internet, or ask older people.

Outcomes

- An interest in the subject encouraged by consulting pupils about their needs.
- Developing trust between the teacher and the pupils, working together and collation skills.
- An indication of the level of knowledge and current needs of the pupils.

Encapsulating our needs

Write your opinions in the capsules below.

1. Drugs – what I know.

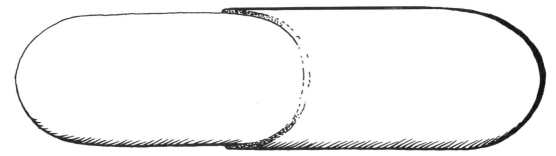

2. Drugs – what I want to find out.

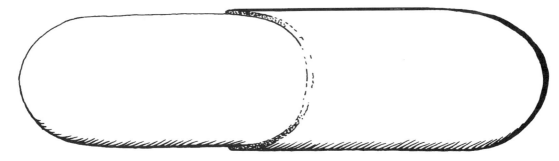

3. Drugs – what my concerns are.

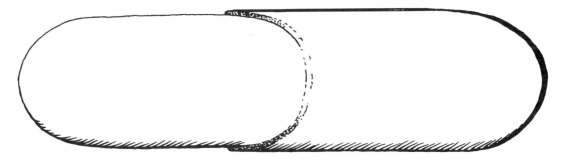

4. Drugs education – what the teacher can do to help.

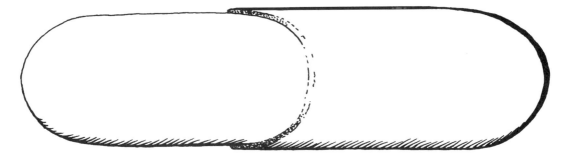

5. Circle the most important factors in each capsule.

ACTIVITY BANK: *Drugs*

Building foundations

Ground rules to enable sensible discussion about drugs

AIMS

To generate ground rules to enable open and sensible discussion about drugs.

Teaching Points

◆ The teacher should inform the pupils of the school's position with regard to confidentiality, contact with parents and anything else appropriate for this subject.
◆ The teacher can contribute relevant rules if the pupils miss them out.
◆ In order for the rules to work, the teacher and the pupils must keep to them.
◆ All the rules need to be agreed by the class and the teacher, before writing them up.
◆ Rules could include:
 – one person to speak at a time
 – everyone has the right to an opinion, and to express it
 – if someone does not want to say anything, they don't have to, and will not be asked why
 – no one will be asked about their own personal experience.

USING THE ACTIVITY SHEET

The focus of the activity is to explore the problems of discussing drugs and to agree on a framework in which the issues can be dealt with openly, honestly and non-judgementally.

Step 1 Tell the class that you want to develop a classroom atmosphere that will enable everyone to feel comfortable discussing drugs. Hand out the activity sheets and ask the pupils, individually and without discussion, to write on the closed doors anything they think would get in the way of an open and helpful class discussion.

Step 2 Split the class into small groups and ask the pupils to share these hindrances and come up with ways to overcome them, writing them inside the building blocks.

Step 3 Ask for a suggestion from each group and negotiate acceptance of it with the whole class. Write it on your own display version of the blocks on a poster. Do the same with others the groups suggest.

Step 4 Ask the pupils their opinions of the rules: whether they can keep to them (what to do if they are broken) and what they think of the process of developing them. Ask the class for a title for the poster. Display it at the beginning of each lesson.

Extension Activities

◆ Ask the pupils to compare the set of ground rules about drugs with another set of rules or laws, such as school rules, age restrictions, the Highway Code, rules for sports and so on.
◆ Ask pupils to research rules that apply in formal situations, for example Parliament, courts, police enquiries and so on. Ask them to list the problems that might occur without these rules.

Outcomes

◆ A set of ground rules to promote open, sensible discussion about drugs, which have been agreed by the class, and which everyone will uphold.
◆ Some understanding of the need for consensus and how to reach it.

Building foundations

1. Write on the closed doors the things that would get in the way of a sensible class discussion about drugs.

2. In your group discuss and write on the building blocks what the members of the class, including your teacher, could do to overcome these hindrances.

Wicked drugs?

Attitudes to drugs

AIMS

To encourage the pupils to consider the range of young people's attitudes to drugs.

Teaching Points

◆ Keep the list of drugs generated for future lessons, continuing to add to and adapt it.

◆ There is no need to try to develop a consensus about which drugs are more dangerous, or to correct information or comment on criteria at this stage. This will be done later.

◆ Try to ensure a range of drugs is included – illegal, legal (for example, alcohol or tobacco), prescribed drugs and over the counter medicines.

◆ Criteria of the danger of drugs include: the proportion of deaths to users, damage to health, knowledge or previous use of drugs, precautions and preparation, reasons for taking them, amount, strength or purity, potential to kill first time, addictive qualities and so on.

◆ Record the reasons given for the dangerousness of each drug.

◆ Keep the poster generated from Step 1 for use in Activity 4 and 7.

USING THE ACTIVITY SHEET

The focus of the activity is to generate a list of all the drugs the pupils know, to compare how dangerous they think they are and the reasons why.

Step 1   Ask the pupils to tell you all the names of drugs they know. Write them on a large piece of paper.

Step 2   Hand out the activity sheets. Ask the pupils to select nine of the drugs and rank them in order of danger, writing the name of the drug in the top half of the box and the reason in the bottom half. Write the names of drugs on individual white cards and fix these to the board. Write 'most dangerous' and 'least dangerous' at opposite ends of the board. Ask individual pupils to suggest where one of the drugs should be on the board and the reason

why. Record their reasons on coloured cards. Do this with every willing member of the class without repeating drugs and without discussion.

Step 3   Ask the class if any of the drugs are in the wrong place. Move the card to where a pupil believes it should be and write the reason for the move on the coloured card.

Step 4   Ask pupils for their criteria for placing the drugs in the continuum and the sources of their information. Make composite lists of their criteria on the board and ask them to write the lists in the second question on their sheets.

Extension Activities

◆ Advise the class to make a note of anything in the lesson that they are unsure of and want to check in future lessons. Ask them to choose one topic to research for presentation to the class.

◆ In groups, ask the pupils to create an open-ended scenario based on one of the dangers of drugs and act it out for the rest of the class.

Outcomes

◆ An understanding that people's attitudes to drugs vary according to a number of factors, including the information they have about them and the source of that information.

◆ An acceptance that everybody has a right to a point of view and to express it.

Wicked drugs?

1. Select nine drugs from the list generated by the class and order them according to how dangerous you think they are. Write the name of the drug in the top part of the box and the reason for its position in the bottom half.

Most dangerous

1.	2.	3.
4.	5.	6.
7.	8.	9.

Least dangerous

2. List all the general criteria that help you to decide how dangerous a drug is. List your sources of information about drugs.

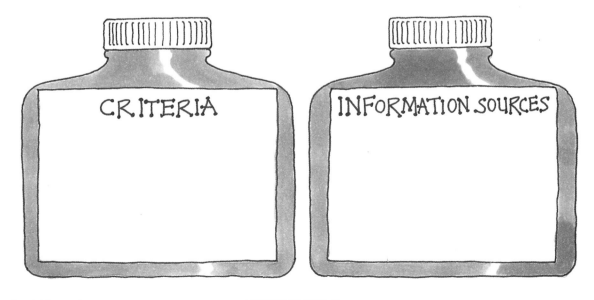

CRITERIA

INFORMATION SOURCES

ACTIVITY BANK: *Drugs*

Designer images

Drug users in the media

— AIMS —

To raise pupil's awareness of how media presentations of drug users may affect their attitudes.

Teaching Points

◆ Drug users are often portrayed in the media as: young, unemployed, homeless, criminal or glamorous.
◆ Drug users may need: drugs, money, help, education, love, support, a home, a job, or alternative medicines to overcome their addiction.
◆ It is important in this activity to attempt to extend and challenge the attitudes of the pupils.
◆ Do not presume that a positive attitude to drug users amongst pupils implies some personal and direct involvement.
◆ There may be a range of attitudes to drug users exhibited by different pupils, from liberal to draconian, but heated debate should not be encouraged.

— USING THE ACTIVITY SHEET —

The focus of the activity is to draw out the perceptions of drug users that the media generates and reinforces, which work against their needs being met.

Step 1   Hand out the activity sheets and ask the pupils, individually, to write in the television screen how drug users are shown in the media, giving them some positive and negative examples. Ask them to feed these back to the class and list them on one side of the board.

Step 2   Divide the class into pairs or small groups and ask them to write around the smiley face the possible needs of a drug user (examples could include types of equipment, as well as emotional support). Collate these needs on the other side of the board.

Step 3   Ask the class to compare and contrast the two lists. Ask why the media take the approach they do. Indicate that the environment generated by the media representation of drug users can make it difficult for them to get what they need. Point out the need for sensible drug education to occur for all, not just for young people.

Step 4   Ask the pupils to decide individually and then to discuss as a class, what is the most difficult problem brought out by this activity, and demonstrate how it could be overcome.

Extension Activities

◆ Ask the pupils to find a story about a drug user in a television programme, film, newspaper or magazine. Tell them to list the positive and negative factors about the drug user that are apparent in the story.
◆ Ask the pupils to write a story about a drug user, in which people's attitudes and actions are positive and helpful.

Outcomes

◆ An understanding that media representation of drug users affects people's attitudes to them.
◆ An understanding that stereotypes created by some examples used by the media may reinforce people's attitudes to drug users.

Designer images

1. Write in the television screen how people who use drugs are portrayed in the media.

2. When your teacher asks you to, write around the smiley face what drug users need to help themselves.

3. What is the most difficult problem brought out by this activity and how can it be overcome?

_____

_____

_____

_____

_____

Uppers and downers

The different categories of drugs

AIMS

To ensure the pupils understand that groups of drugs have different effects.

Teaching Points

◆ Drugs that stimulate the nervous system, known as stimulants or 'uppers', include: amphetamines, cocaine and crack, caffeine, tobacco and nicotine, anabolic steroids, alkyl (amyl and butyl) nitrites ('poppers'), hallucinogenic amphetamines (ecstasy) and khat.

◆ Drugs that depress the nervous system are known as depressants, sedatives or 'downers' and include: alcohol, barbiturates, benzodiazepines/minor tranquillizers (Valium, Librium, Ativan, Mogadon, Temazepam or 'jellies'), GHB, solvents, gases and aerosols. It is important to note that depressants do not make you feel depressed.

◆ Drugs that alter perceptual function, called hallucinogens, include: LSD, hallucinogenic ('magic') mushrooms, cannabis, DMT and Ketamine.

◆ Drugs that reduce pain are called analgesics, e.g. heroin, opium, morphine, methadone, pethidine and codeine.

◆ Some drugs appear to have the effects of drugs in other categories, e.g. smoking cigarettes may calm people's nerves; alcohol may initially make some people more active; cannabis is usually smoked for its relaxing effects. Most analgesics will have a depressant effect, especially if there is no physical pain.

◆ Keep the activity sheet for use in Activity 16.

USING THE ACTIVITY SHEET

The focus of the activity is to find out if the pupils know to which categories different drugs belong and to provide them with information.

Step 1   Display the list of drugs from Activity 3. Inform the pupils that when people take drugs for non-medical reasons, they do so for the effect of the drug. Explain the four terms depressant, stimulant, hallucinogen and analgesic. Hand out the activity sheets and ask the pupils to transfer the names of the drugs into the appropriate faces.

Step 2   Draw the faces on the board and go through all the drugs, ensuring the pupils have them in the right positions.

Step 3   Divide the class into pairs, or small groups, and ask them to list the reasons why people might take the drugs in each category and collate their responses on the board.

Step 4   Ask the pupils to write on their activity sheets one thing they have learned in this activity, and one thing that was reinforced. They may feed this back to the class if they wish.

Extension Activities

◆ Ask the pupils to make a list of the activities that a drug user might do and activities that they might find difficult, or be dangerous, while under the influence of drugs.

◆ Discuss as a class situations that might make you feel more awake, more relaxed, alter your perceptions, or reduce pain.

Outcomes

◆ An understanding of the effects of different categories of drugs and of which drugs are in each category.

◆ Some understanding of the reasons why people might take different types of drugs.

Uppers and downers

1. Write the names of drugs in the boxes under the appropriate faces.

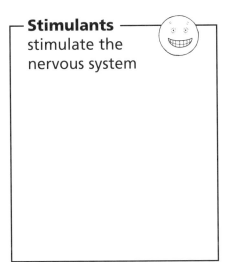

Stimulants
stimulate the
nervous system

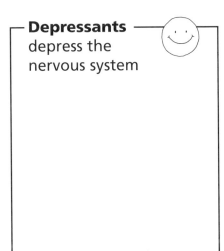

Depressants
depress the
nervous system

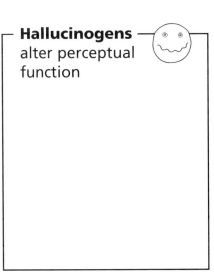

Hallucinogens
alter perceptual
function

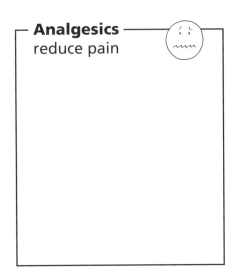

Analgesics
reduce pain

Don't know

2. Why would people want to take these groups of drugs?

 Stimulants _____

 Depressants _____

 Hallucinogens _____

 Analgesics _____

3. Write down one thing you have learned in this activity. _____

_____

4. Write one thing you knew already. _____

_____

Have you got the knowledge?

Information about drugs

AIMS

To ensure the pupils have accurate, comprehensive and unbiased information about drugs.

Teaching Points

Materials needed
Leaflets about drugs. These can be obtained from Health Promotion Units.

◆ The drugs most commonly used by young people, are: tobacco, alcohol, cannabis, amphetamines, solvents, 'poppers', LSD, 'magic' mushrooms and ecstasy.
◆ Be prepared for variations of knowledge between pupils' personal experience based on different sources of information, ranging from parents, the media, leaflets and so on.
◆ Information about drugs is not always consistent between supposedly reliable sources. Take into account the apparent reasons for presenting the information and consider if it is accurate, comprehensive and unbiased and if not why not.
◆ There may be questions and debatable information that you are not able to resolve in the lesson. Attempt to research any questions for the next lesson, or ask the pupils to. See page 55 for reliable contacts.
◆ Try to ensure the information you give is not affected by your attitudes to specific drugs, or by the way you present it.

USING THE ACTIVITY SHEET

The focus of the activity is for the pupils to check their knowledge and to find out what they want to know about the drugs they have heard of.

Step 1   With the class, select six drugs on which to focus. Hand out the activity sheets. Using one of the six drugs, ask the pupils to complete the first two questions on the activity sheet.

Step 2   Arrange the pupils into groups examining the same drug and give each group an extra sheet on which to collate their contributions. Pass the sheets around the groups, asking new groups to add to the sheet, by ticking what they think is correct, putting a cross against what they think is wrong, answering questions if they can and adding anything else.

Step 3   Return the sheets to the original groups and hand out appropriate copies of the drug files and other reliable sources of information. The task of each group is to check the information, find answers to the questions and to give a short presentation about their drug.

Step 4   Ask the pupils to review the information and questions on their original sheets and to answer the last question on the activity sheet.

Extension Activities

◆ Help the pupils to use the Internet to research a drug from this activity, to resolve any debatable information, or a drug not covered in the lesson.
◆ Invite a guest speaker from one of the local agencies to come and talk to the class.

Outcomes

◆ An understanding that reliability of drug information varies according to its source.
◆ The pupils have received information about relevant drugs that is as correct, comprehensive, and unbiased as is possible.

Have you got the knowledge?

Name of drug: _____

1. Write in the book what you know, or think you know, about this drug.

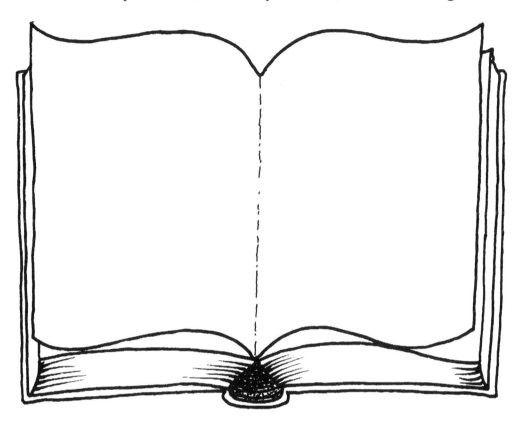

2. Write next to the question marks what you would like to know about this drug.

_____ **?**
_____ **?**
_____ **?**
_____ **?**
_____ **?**

3. Place a tick or cross against the details you wrote in the book, indicating whether they were correct or not. Write the answers to the questions that you wanted to ask on the back of the sheet.

4. Write down one thing you have learned about the other drugs covered in this activity.

_____
_____
_____
_____

Drug talk

Words used about drugs and drug use

── AIMS ──

To develop the pupils' understanding of the terminology associated with drug use.

Teaching Points

◆ There are many different words for the same drug, particularly cannabis, some of which are very parochial. Consult the local police and drug counselling agency, as well as the information sources detailed on page 55, to generate a comprehensive list.

◆ The pupils may come up with words you are unsure of. Use one of the above information sources and the drug files at the back of the book to help the pupils check these as soon as possible.

◆ The following words are listed in the SCAA example drug education programme: abuse, addiction, adulteration, dependence, misuse, overdose, tolerance, withdrawal. Ensure the pupils know their meanings (definitions are provided in the glossary on page 54).

── USING THE ACTIVITY SHEET ──

The focus of this activity is to ensure that the pupils know the different names for the same drug and understand some of the more technical drug terminology.

Step 1   Display the list of drugs from Activity 3, or generate a list of all the names of drugs the pupils know. Hand out the activity sheets and ask the pupils, working individually, to sort the list into words for the same drug and write these under the relevant picture. Take the drugs one at a time and list the alternative names on the board. Ensure that the pupils have the correct ones on their sheets.

Step 2   Ask the class to tell you other words they have heard used about drugs and write them on the board. Ask them to write them on their activity sheets in the appropriate places.

Step 3   Divide the class into small groups. Ask each group to compare their lists and encourage them to help each other with the meanings. Hand out a copy of the glossary to each group to help them check their understanding of a drug term.

Step 4   Encourage the groups to feed back any problems. Ask them to note the meanings of three words they have learned. Agree with the class on a list of universally understood words that will be used in future lessons.

Extension Activities

◆ Encourage the pupils to use a variety of sources of information to find out additional names for the drugs. Compile a class information sheet of any further names for drugs found.

◆ Invite the pupils to look in magazines and newspapers for words covered in this lesson to see if they are used correctly. Note other words that were not part of the activity.

Outcomes

◆ A knowledge of the different words used for the same drug.

◆ An understanding of some of the more technical drug terms.

◆ Development of cooperating skills in helping others to understand the meanings of words.

Drug talk

1. Write the different names for the same drug in the appropriate places.

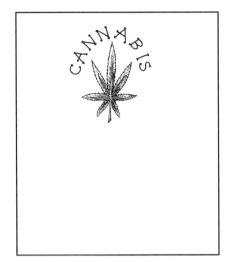 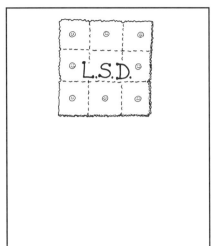 

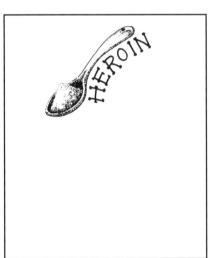  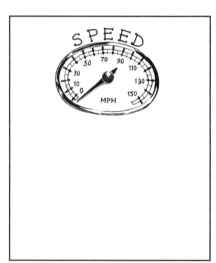

2. Write the words whose meanings you are sure you know in the left side of the capsule and the ones about which you are unsure in the right side.

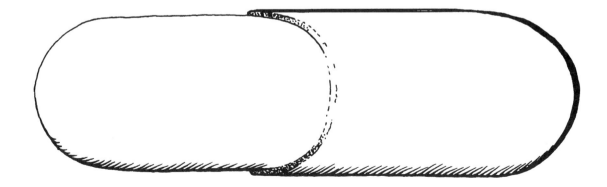

3. On the back of the sheet, write down the meanings of three words you have learned in this activity.

ACTIVITY BANK: *Drugs*

What is allowed?

The laws about drugs

AIMS

To ensure the pupils understand the drug laws.

Teaching Points

- ◆ The laws on drugs are complex, inconsistent and not always related to substantiated dangers.
- ◆ Alcohol laws are dealt with in more detail in *Activity Bank: Alcohol*.
- ◆ The supply of drugs refers to both giving someone an illegal drug and selling it to them.
- ◆ There is an additional offence of 'possession with intent to supply', to cover people caught in possession of large quantities of illegal drugs, but not in the act of supplying them.
- ◆ The way the law is implemented, and the penalties imposed, vary across the country. The local police, particularly the community or schools liaison department, will be able to provide appropriate information.
- ◆ See the drug files and page 53 for additional information about the legal position of some of the drugs.

USING THE ACTIVITY SHEET

The focus of this activity is to find out what the pupils know about the drug laws and to correct their information if they are wrong.

Step 1   Ask the pupils to tell you what they think the range of offences are in relation to drugs. Write the correct ones on the board. Display the list of drugs from Activity 3, or generate a list of all the names of drugs the pupils know.

Step 2   Hand out the activity sheets and, as an individual activity, ask the pupils to write the drugs in the appropriate places. Split the class into small groups to compare their sheets and answer the question about classes of drugs.

Step 3   Give each group a copy of 'The drug laws' to check their knowledge against and to correct their sheets. Ask them to mention anything that is unclear.

Step 4   Ask a few specific questions to review their work, for example 'What can make a Class B drug into a Class A drug?' Ask each group to prepare a question for the others to answer.

Extension Activities

- ◆ Invite your local police representative, community or schools liaison department to present a talk on the drug laws and what happens to offenders in your area.
- ◆ Ask the pupils to write a story in which someone accidentally, or unknowingly, breaks a drug law and receives a warning from the police, rather than being prosecuted.

Outcomes

- ◆ An understanding of the range of drug laws and of which drugs are illegal.
- ◆ Development of analysing skills associated with checking information.

What is allowed?

1. With which drugs is it an offence to do the following:

Possess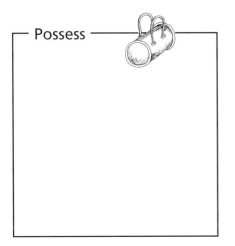

Supply
(sell or give)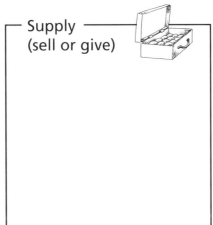

Produce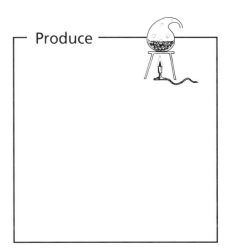

Import/
export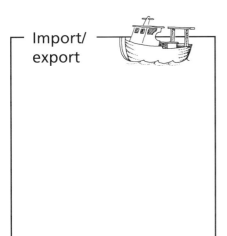

Drive under
the
influence of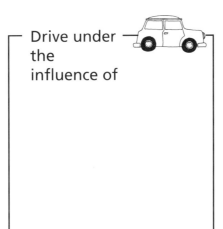

Allow premises
to be used for
their use, supply
or production

2. The Misuse of Drugs Act 1971, categorises illegal drugs into three classes, according to how dangerous it is thought they are. Class A is the most dangerous with the highest penalties. Which drugs do you think are in each class?

Class A _____

Class B _____

Class C _____

3. Devise a question on the laws about drugs to ask another group.

_____

_____

_____

Where do you stand?

Attitudes to drug laws

— AIMS —

To raise pupils' awareness of their own opinions and those of others towards current drug laws.

Teaching Points

Materials needed

Prepared sheets of paper with 'Strongly agree', 'Agree', 'Don't know', 'Disagree' and 'Strongly disagree' on them and a way of distributing them along a continuum in the classroom.

◆ Try not to allow vociferous arguments to continue so that they adversely affect the atmosphere of the lesson.
◆ There are no correct answers; everyone has the right to have and express his or her point of view.
◆ See the drug files and page 53 for additional information about the legal position on drugs.

— USING THE ACTIVITY SHEET —

The focus of the activity is to give the pupils the opportunity to comment on the current drug laws and to consider other people's attitudes to them.

Step 1 Hand out the activity sheets and ask the pupils to complete them individually. Put up the continuum notices.

Step 2 Select a statement from the activity sheet. Ask the pupils to stand in the appropriate place in the continuum and ask volunteers to give their reasons for their opinion. Do the same for another statement and ask volunteers to try to persuade other pupils to move. Continue with the statements until you have used sufficient in the time available. Ask for volunteers to read out their statements and the pupils to move into the continuum position they believe is appropriate.

Step 3 Ask for volunteers to take the roles of a range of adults (e.g. police officer, politician, teacher, doctor, cannabis smoker, ecstasy user, heroin injector, parent) and repeat one or two of the statements. Ask volunteers to contemplate why that adult might have such an opinion and whether they agree with them.

Step 4 Ask the pupils to tell you one law they are happy with and one they would like to change or introduce and say why they think any one law has been made.

Extension Activities

◆ Ask pupils to collect responses to the statements on the activity sheet from twenty adults and twenty young people. The final results should be presented in a chart or graph form and the results compared.
◆ Ask pupils to collect topical or local issues to make additional statements to the activity and record their responses.

Outcomes

◆ Development of analysing skills in considering pupils' own attitudes to drug laws and emphasising skills in considering those of others.
◆ Development of debating skills.

Where do you stand?

1. Tick the box according to your views on these statements and write your reason.

	Strongly agree	Agree	Don't know	Disagree	Strongly disagree
We need laws to control the use of drugs.	☐	☐	☐	☐	☐

Reason: _____

The laws about alcohol are sensible.	☐	☐	☐	☐	☐

Reason: _____

The law on tobacco needs to be changed.	☐	☐	☐	☐	☐

Reason: _____

Cannabis should be legalised.	☐	☐	☐	☐	☐

Reason: _____

Heroin should be legalised.	☐	☐	☐	☐	☐

Reason: _____

The drug laws in all the countries of the world should be the same.	☐	☐	☐	☐	☐

Reason: _____

2. Make up your own statement about drug laws to be debated.

_____

_____

_____

3. Which drug law would you like to change or introduce? Explain why you think any one drug law exists.

_____

_____

_____

School rules about drugs

You need to know what they are

— AIMS —

To ensure the pupils know the school rules and procedures about drugs.

Teaching Points

Materials needed
A copy of the school drug policy (simplify it if necessary) for the pupils.

◆ The school deals with incidents involving drugs in a caring, fair and consistent manner.
◆ The pupils may not agree with all the school rules but have to accept them; but there may be a structure for consultation, for example a school council.
◆ School rules and procedures should cover: bringing drugs into school; procedures for dealing with a pupil under the influence; supplying illegal drugs; medical emergencies; a range of responses for different drug-related incidents, to include welfare as well as sanctions; parental and police involvement; use of drugs on the school premises; allegations, suspicion and disclosure; confidentiality.
◆ School rules for alcohol are dealt with in detail in *Activity Bank: Alcohol*.

USING THE ACTIVITY SHEET

The focus of the activity is to enable the pupils to understand the school rules about drugs and the reasons for them, starting with their own views.

Step 1   Distribute the activity sheets and divide the class into five groups. Give each group a different type of incident to consider and ask them to discuss and write down how they think each of the people detailed should respond to, or be involved in, an incident of that nature.

Step 2   Take feedback from each group, writing relevant elements on the board. As more incidents are discussed, try to elicit some general principles that could apply to all types of incidents, (e.g. fairness, assessment of the situation before reacting).

Step 3   Explain the school rules and procedures about drugs and the reasons for them. Discuss with the class the relationship between the classwork and the reality. Ask the pupils to write the reasons on their sheet.

Step 4   Ask the groups to compare the school rules with the suggestions they generated, and to feed back one positive aspect of the school rules and one aspect they are not entirely happy with.

Extension Activities

◆ Ask pupils to consider the school rules about drugs in relation to the law (see the drug files and page 53).
◆ Consider, with the class, the similarities and differences between the school rules about illegal drugs and those about medicines, alcohol and mobile phones and the reasons for them.

Outcomes

◆ A knowledge of the school rules about drugs and the reasons for them.
◆ An understanding that some rules may not be negotiable and the consequences of breaking them.
◆ Evaluating responses to a range of drug-related incidents.

School rules about drugs

1. Circle the type of drug incident the teacher asks your group to consider.

   A pupil under the influence.
   A pupil in possession of an illegal drug.
   A pupil supplying illegal drugs.
   A medical emergency.
   A pupil expressing concern about another's drug use.

   Write in the boxes how you would like the following people to respond to, or be involved with, this type of incident.

Other pupils

Teachers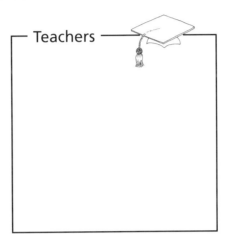

Parents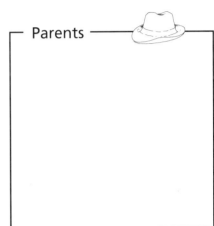

Police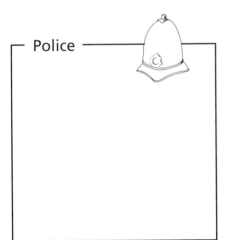

Doctors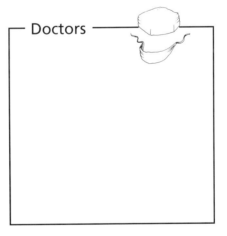

Others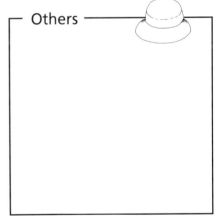

2. What are the general principles that should apply to all drug incidents?

   _____

   _____

   _____

3. Copy the school rules about drugs, on to the back of your sheet.

It won't happen to me!

The risks of taking drugs

AIMS

To explore the risks associated with taking drugs.

Teaching Points

◆ Ensure pupils do not work on the same drug as they worked on in Activity 6.
◆ The general risk of taking any drug is that the short-term effects are unpredictable, as they may vary according to: the drug; the amount taken and over what period of time; its strength; familiarity with that drug; where, when, how and with whom the drug is taken; the mood and expectations of the user; or unknown medical or physical factors.
◆ Long-term risks include a variety of social, physical, financial, personal and psychological problems.
◆ The general risks of taking illegal drugs also include: the consequences of doing something illegal and the lack of certainty that the drug is what the supplier says it is.

USING THE ACTIVITY SHEET

The focus of the activity is for the pupils to comment on the risks they think are apparent with taking a range of drugs, to correct their information and to consider the general risks of taking any drug.

Step 1   Ask the pupils to select six drugs they want to consider the risks of taking. Arrange the pupils into six groups and apportion the name of a drug to each group. Hand out the activity sheets and ask the pupils to write the physical risks inside the figure and other risks outside it.

Step 2   Hand out copies of the appropriate drug file to each group, to check their information against.

Step 3   Write the names of the drugs as headings on the board. Ask each group to suggest one risk for their drug; other groups can also indicate if previous risks apply to their drug as well. Ensure that all the risks for all the drugs are detailed. Reinforce the risks that apply to all drugs or all illegal drugs.

Step 4   Ask the pupils to mark the risks on their sheets according to the instructions and to feed back the greatest risk in taking their drug and for taking any drug.

Extension Activities

◆ Ask the pupils to write a mock interview in which two people took the same risk with a drug, but the results were different.
◆ Ask the pupils to list other activities for which the same risks apply as for all drugs, or all illegal drugs.

Outcomes

◆ An increased understanding of the range of risks associated with taking any drugs, illegal drugs and specific drugs.
◆ Development of prioritising and cooperating skills.

It won't happen to me!

Drug: _____

1. Write inside the outline of the figure the physical risks of taking this drug. Outside of it , write the other risks.

2. Compare your risks with the drug file information. Cross out the ones that are not mentioned, add the ones you left out and leave those that are correct.

3. Draw a circle round the risks that apply to all drugs and a square round the ones that apply to illegal drugs.

4. What is the greatest risk in taking:

   any drug?   _____

   illegal drugs?   _____

   this drug?   _____

Yes I will! No I won't!

Decision-making and assertiveness in drug situations

— AIMS —

To consider how best to communicate a decision about drug-taking.

Teaching Points

- Being aggressive means saying what you want without caring about other people's feelings. This often produces an aggressive reaction.
- Being passive means not saying what you want to, perhaps hoping that others will guess, which can have the effect of not getting what you want.
- Being assertive means saying what you want in a straightforward, open and direct way. This means you do what you want to do, but there is less chance of upsetting other people and of regretting your decision or the way you communicated it.
- Factors that affect decision-making about drugs include: information, fear, other people's views and influence, health risks, the law, previous experience, and curiosity.

— USING THE ACTIVITY SHEET —

The focus of the activity is to use possible drug situations to consider aggressive, passive and assertive behaviour and the effect it has on others.

Step 1   Write the words 'aggressive', 'passive' and 'assertive' on the board and ensure that the pupils know what they mean. Split the class into five groups. Hand out the activity sheets, two for each group and one for each pupil. Ask each group to work on one of the situations.

Step 2   Ask the groups to work through their situations for a 'yes' response, noting on different group sheets the factors taken into account, the decision, the three different ways of communicating it and the other person's

reaction. Then ask the pupils to do the same exercise with a 'no' response.

Step 3   Ask the groups to present their two best dialogues, ensuring both decisions and all three types of response are included.

Step 4   Make a combined list of all the decision-making factors and make generalisations about them for the pupils to note on their own sheets. Do the same for the three types of response and others' reactions.

Extension Activities

- Ask the pupils to choose another situation from the activity sheet. They should write an internal monologue, detailing the person's thoughts about the decision, how they are going to communicate it, and their concerns about others' responses.
- Ask pupils to make three lists of situations in which they or others were aggressive, passive or assertive.

Outcomes

- An understanding of aggressive, passive and assertive behaviour and how people react to such behaviour.
- An understanding of the factors to take into account in drug situations.

Yes I will! No I won't!

Circle the type of situation the teacher asks you to consider.

A friend offers a cigarette.

An older relative offers an alcoholic drink.

A younger friend wants you to sniff solvents with them.

Your brother or sister suggests you take their medicine.

An older friend offers you some cannabis.

1. The factors to take into account when deciding:

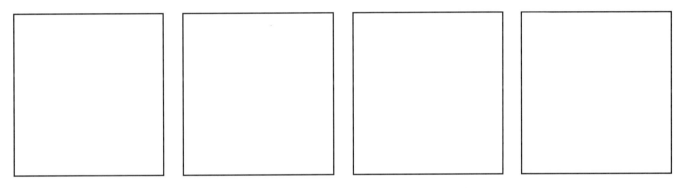

2. The decision:

3. The response: Aggressive   Assertive   Passive

4. The reaction:

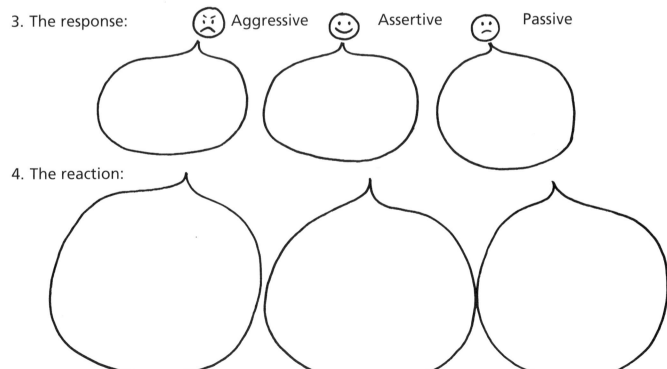

Enhancing performance?

To raise the issues of drug-taking in sport

AIMS

To raise the issues of drug-taking in sport.

Teaching Points

These are the common drugs banned in most sports:

◆ Stimulants – used in long-distance events (e.g. cycling and skiing) and in sports where aggression may help (e.g. American football).
◆ Analgesics – used when the pain of injury is stopping somebody taking part in sport.
◆ Anabolic steroids – used in sports where muscle bulk is important (e.g. body-building, throwing events).
◆ Beta blockers – used in sports where a steady hand and eye are essential (e.g. archery).
◆ Diuretics – used in sports with weight categories (e.g. boxing, weightlifting). They cause loss of water and therefore weight. They can also help get rid of traces of other banned drugs in the urine. Excessive fluid loss can cause dizziness, fainting, muscle cramp, headache, feeling sick and vomiting. It can also damage the heart and the kidneys.

USING THE ACTIVITY SHEET

The focus of the activity is to consider what types of drug may enhance performance in particular sports, the reasons why people might take them, and the general question of whether sportspeople should be allowed to use any drugs.

Step 1   Hand out the activity sheets and ask the pupils to list, individually, the sports in which the drugs listed on their sheet might be taken to improve performance.

Step 2   Write the names of the drugs on the board and make a composite list of the sports for each drug. Ask for generalisations about the types of sport that appear under each drug.

Step 3   Split the class into small groups and ask them to list the reasons why individuals might, or might not, take drugs to improve their performance.

Step 4   Write the following question on the board 'If drug abuse is unavoidable, why not allow complete freedom of drug use and let the competitor choose?' Debate the question and write the arguments on the board. Ask pupils to complete the last part of the activity sheet.

Extension Activities

◆ Ask the pupils to write to the governing body of a sport in which they are interested, asking for information on which substances are banned and why.
◆ Invite the pupils to conduct a questionnaire asking a number of adults what they do that is legal to enhance their health, or their performance in work, or their social life. The final results should be presented in a graph.

Outcomes

◆ An understanding of the use of drugs in sport to enhance performance.
◆ Analysing the reasons why people take drugs for sporting reasons and why others object.
◆ Development of debating skills.

Enhancing performance?

1. In which sports might these drugs be misused?

Stimulants – reduce tiredness; increase alertness, confidence, determination, aggression; make people feel stronger.

_____

_____

Anabolic steroids – similar to some natural hormones. They help to build muscle and increase aggression.

_____

_____

Beta blockers – counteract adrenaline (a hormone in the body) helping to calm people down.

_____

_____

Diuretics – remove liquid from the body by increasing urination.

_____

_____

2a. Why do some people take drugs to improve performance?

_____

_____

2b. Why do some people choose not to take drugs to improve performance?

_____

_____

3. If drug abuse is unavoidable, why not allow complete freedom of drug use and let the competitor choose whether or not to take drugs? Use the back of the sheet for your answer.

ACTIVITY BANK: _Drugs_

Kids today!

Role models

AIMS

To consider the effects on children of older people's legal drug use.

Teaching Points

◆ Young people tend to find it easy to make suggestions for advice for younger children, but do not necessarily realise or accept that it could apply to them as well.
◆ Their advice can be quite polarised, extreme, even draconian and may need to be tempered.
◆ An understanding that everyone is responsible for their own actions starts to develop at about the age of nine and may still not be fully developed by the age of 14.
◆ It is helpful for young people if the adults they are in contact with (including teachers) behave consistently with the suggestions they make for others.

USING THE ACTIVITY SHEET

The focus of the activity is to consider messages about legal drugs to convey to younger children and how people's actions can reinforce or contradict them.

Step 1   Hand out the activity sheets and drug files and (as an individual activity) ask the pupils to write, inside the appropriate drawing, a simple message for younger children about that particular drug. Copy the drawings on the board and list the messages, marking repeats.

Step 2   Divide the class into eight groups, two groups for each drug, ensuring that all are covered. Ask one group in each pair to develop a story in which the message is reinforced by an older person and ask the other group to develop a story in which the message is

contradicted. In both stories the older person must take responsibility for their actions.

Step 3   Ask the pairs of groups to present their stories, asking the others to extract general issues raised about role models and taking responsibility. Write the issues on the board.

Step 4   Ask the groups to write suggestions for how people of their own age can take responsibility for their actions and offer positive role models to younger children.

Extension Activities

◆ Invite the pupils to compile a list of people who present positive and negative role models. They should be able to comment on the qualities the role models demonstrate, that the pupils admire or dislike.
◆ Ask the pupils to write about a recent occasion when they or someone else took, or didn't take, responsibility for their actions and the effects this had on them and other people.

Outcomes

◆ An understanding of the effects of people's behaviour on others, especially younger people.
◆ An understanding of the benefits of taking responsibility for one's own behaviour.

Kids today!

1. Write a simple message for younger children in these drawings of legal drugs:

Medicines

Tobacco

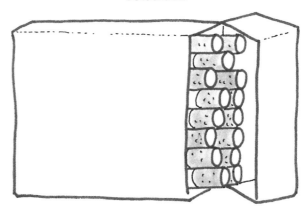

Alcohol

Solvents

2. Develop a story in which one of the messages is reinforced, or contradicted, by an older person, who takes responsibility for their actions.

_____

_____

_____

_____

3. How can people of your own age take responsibility for their actions and offer positive role models to younger children?

_____

_____

Safety last?

Taking responsibility for one's own and others' safety

AIMS

To generate a set of safety 'rules' to apply to any drug-taking situation.

Teaching Points

Safety rules for the use of any legal or illegal drug could include:

◆ Ensure one person is not under the influence, in order to deal with any problems, and keep in mind people and places you can go to for help if needed.
◆ If you don't want to take something or feel you have had enough – don't.
◆ If there are any medical difficulties, get help immediately and tell the truth about what has been taken.
◆ Don't take drugs in places that are dangerous in themselves.
◆ Be aware of specific problems with particular drugs or combinations of drugs, and always use the safest way of taking them.
◆ The safest thing to do is not take any drug.

USING THE ACTIVITY SHEET

The focus of this activity is to consider the immediate dangers in taking drugs and to acknowledge that, despite the law and common sense, people misuse drugs and to use a fictitious scenario to generate safety 'rules'.

Step 1   Hand out the activity sheets and (as an individual activity) ask the pupils to list the possible immediate dangers of taking any drug. List the reasons on the board.

Step 2   Divide the class into five groups and give each group the names of a type of drug to consider, either alcohol, solvents, cannabis, amphetamines or LSD. Ask the groups to devise a scenario in which there is a safety issue with regard to the drug.

Step 3   Hand out the appropriate drug files to the pupils and ask the groups to read them and list what individuals in their scenario could do to take responsibility for their own and others' safety.

Step 4   Ask the groups to feed the precautions back to the rest of the class. With the whole class, negotiate some general safety 'rules' that can be applied to any drug-taking situation. Ask the pupils to write the final list on their sheets and remind them that the safest rule is not to take any drug.

Extension Activities

◆ Compare the drug safety rules with those used for other activities, for example throwing events in athletics, swimming, driving, outdoor expeditions, camping and so on.
◆ Ask the pupils to list occasions and actions when they or someone else has, or has not, taken responsibility for their own or other people's safety, and how they felt.

Outcomes

◆ A list of general safety rules to apply to any situation in which the pupils might come across drugs.
◆ An increased awareness of safety in drug-taking situations where drugs are used.

Safety last?

1. Complete this notice:

+---+
| |
| WARNING |
| THE DANGERS OF TAKING DRUGS ARE: |
| |
| |
| |
| |
| BY ORDER S.P. LIFF |
+---+

2. Develop a scenario in which there is a safety issue with the drug.

    _____

    _____

    _____

3a. What could you do to take responsibility for your own safety in this situation?

    _____

    _____

    _____

3b. What could you do to take responsibility for the safety of others in this situation?

    _____

    _____

    _____

4. Our safety rules for drug-taking are:

    _____

    _____

    _____

Help! Now!

Assisting a friend under the influence of drugs

AIMS

To alert pupils to action to help someone under the influence of drugs.

Teaching Points

◆ People under the influence of drugs may not be able, nor want, to do what is best for them.
◆ Do not administer first aid unless you are absolutely sure of what you are doing and do not give the drug-taker anything to take to relieve their symptoms.
◆ The best thing to do is to seek help from a responsible adult.
◆ Find out from a trained first-aider the current recommended recovery position.
◆ The health and safety of the person is more important than whether you think anyone will get into trouble.
◆ If the person is unwell and you are asked what they have taken, be completely honest.
◆ If the person is anxious or upset, try to reassure them.
◆ Refer to the school policy and procedures about dealing with intoxication.

USING THE ACTIVITY SHEET

The focus of the activity is to consider the problems that might arise when someone is under the influence of drugs. It also aims to generate pupils' ideas about how to cope with these problems and then to inform them of the best course of action.

Step 1   Briefly, revise the four categories of drugs in Activity 5. Hand out the activity sheets and, as an individual activity, ask the pupils to complete the first section. They should refer to the appropriate drug files. Collate their responses on the board under the headings.

Step 2   Split the class into four groups and give each group one of the categories to work on. Ask the pupils to complete the second section and to consider what could be done to help someone who is suffering from the problems listed on the board.

Step 3   Write down the pupils' suggestions on the board, leading the discussion to consideration of the safest and simplest course of action to take. Refer to the teaching points for guidance and, if necessary, write the guidelines on the board.

Step 4   Ask the groups to consider their original suggestions, to tick the appropriate ones and to cross out those that are inappropriate, before copying what is on the board. Inform them of the school policy and procedures for dealing with intoxication.

Extension Activities

◆ Ask pupils to find out how police, doctors, nurses and a drug agency can help someone under the influence of drugs and what others can do in support.
◆ Find out from a first-aider the ABC of first aid and the recovery position. Present the information to the class and demonstrate the position on a volunteer.

Outcomes

◆ An understanding of the problems associated with the different categories of drugs.
◆ Some knowledge of the appropriate action to take when helping with someone who is under the influence of drugs.
◆ Development of evaluating and prioritising skills.

Help! Now!

1. What are the possible problems if someone takes different drugs?

STIMULANTS	DEPRESSANTS
ANY DRUG	
HALLUCINOGENS	ANALGESICS

2. How can someone under the influence of _____ be helped?

_____

_____

_____

3. What is the most helpful thing you can do for someone under the influence of drugs?

_____

_____

_____

_____

Tell me about it

Communicating about drugs with peers, parents and professionals

AIMS

To explore the problems and solutions of talking about drugs with a range of people.

Teaching Points

Materials needed
It would be useful to obtain copies of the free HEA publication *A Parent's Guide to Drugs and Alcohol*, which gives advice on talking about drugs with children (it is available from the Drug Campaign Information Service (DCIS) on 01304 614 731).

◆ Young people may feel inhibited talking to others about drugs because of: the legal situation; fears of over-reaction and punishment; ignorance of some adults about drugs or concern that initiating a discussion may be interpreted as current involvement.
◆ Adults might be affected by: ignorance and misinformation; the legal position; suspicions; their responsibilities.
◆ Discussion about drugs can be improved if people: are open and honest about their feelings, thoughts and responsibilities; think before they react; inform themselves about drugs in the lives of young people; listen carefully to what is actually being said without making presumptions.

USING THE ACTIVITY SHEET

The focus of the activity is to use the thoughts and feelings that young people experience when talking with others about drugs, and to consider how these situations could be improved.

Step 1 Hand out the activity sheets and ask the pupils to consider, working individually, what they might feel, think and say if they wanted to start a discussion about drugs with people their own age, parents and professionals (they may need some help and stimulus with the 'feeling' words). Collate on the board their responses for feelings and thoughts.

Step 2 Split the class into six groups, two each to focus on peers, parents and professionals. Ask them to list the problems that affect talking

about drugs with those people and what each could do to improve the situation.

Step 3 Ask the groups to feed their work back to the class and try to generalise the problems and solutions.

Step 4 Ask the groups to consider what parents and professionals might feel, think and say if a young person initiated a discussion about drugs with them.

Extension Activities

◆ Ask the pupils to write a letter to a friend, parent or professional, indicating that they want to talk to the reader about drugs, the difficulties they envisage and what they could do to help.
◆ Compare the suggestions about how parents can talk to their children about drugs with advice from magazines and other sources.

Outcomes

◆ An understanding of the difficulties inherent in talking to other people about drugs and possible ways to overcome them.
◆ Development of empathising skills through consideration of other people's feelings and thoughts.

Tell me about it

1. What would your feelings and thoughts be and what would you say, if you wanted to start a conversation about drugs with the following people:

	Feelings	**Thoughts**	**Words**

Someone your age

Parent

Police officer, teacher or doctor

2. What are the problems in talking about drugs with peers, parents or professionals?

_____

_____

3a. What could you do to improve the situation?

_____

_____

3b. What could they do to improve the situation?

_____

_____

4. What might parents and professionals feel, think and say if a young person initiated a discussion about drugs with them?

_____

_____

Can I help you?

Local and national advice and support

AIMS

To alert pupils to the advice and support that is available locally and nationally.

Teaching Points

Materials needed

The National Drugs Helpline (0800 77 66 00) offers information and free confidential advice and leaflets. Obtain information about the local drug agency, not just where it is but also what services it offers; especially to young people.

The free HEA publication for 11–14-year olds called *Drugs: the facts* can be obtained from DCIS by phoning 01304 614731 (multiple copies) or The National Drugs Helpline (single copies).

◆ Counselling agencies only work with volunteer drug users and are likely to encourage them to explore and understand their situation before deciding on appropriate action.

◆ Most young people who take (illegal) drugs do not see their drug useage as a problem.

◆ Young people prefer advice and support about drugs to be available anonymously and from places they tend to frequent for other, more general reasons.

USING THE ACTIVITY SHEET

The focus of the activity is to consider the problems that users of drugs might have, how they could be dealt with, and to provide information about the services available.

Step 1   List the drugs in the drug files on the board. Apportion, or ask pupils to select a drug to work on, ensuring that the range includes alcohol, cannabis, solvents, amphetamines, LSD, 'magic' mushrooms and 'poppers'. Ask the pupils, as an individual activity, to list the kinds of information, support and advice that a person taking that drug might seek.

Step 2   Ask pairs of pupils focusing on the same drug to compare notes. Hand out the appropriate drug files for pupils to check their answers against. Join pairs with different drugs and ask them to generalise their suggestions and to write their suggestions under question 2. Collate their suggestions on the board.

Step 3   Ask the quartets to consider the best criteria for meeting the needs of drug users: for example, who, where and when or other relevant factors.

Step 4   Ask the groups to feed their criteria back to the class and give them any information about local and national advice and support you have available.

Extension Activities

◆ Ask the pupils, in pairs, to write a letter about a drug problem to a magazine agony aunt or uncle and the reply. Compare it with real ones in young people's magazines.

◆ Invite a local youth worker, or drug counsellor, to tell you about his or her work.

Outcomes

◆ Some knowledge of the problems associated with specific drugs.

◆ Evaluating the nature of advice and support required to attend to these problems.

◆ Knowledge of information about local and national advice and support.

Can I help you?

1. Write under the drawings the kinds of information, support and advice a user of
_____ might seek.

Information	**Support**	**Advice**

_____	_____	_____
_____	_____	_____
_____	_____	_____
_____	_____	_____

2. What kinds of information, support and advice might **any** drug users seek?

Information	**Support**	**Advice**
_____	_____	_____
_____	_____	_____
_____	_____	_____
_____	_____	_____

3. Write down what factors will ensure that the information, support and advice is appropriate.

_____

_____

_____

_____

_____

Absolutely spliffing!

Course evaluation

— AIMS —

To review and evaluate the drug education programme.

Teaching Points

Materials needed
Four large sheets of paper or equivalent, each one headed with one of the categories on the activity sheet.

◆ The sheet from Activity 1, which detailed the pupils needs in drug education, is required for this activity.
◆ If the pupil sheets for other activities have been saved, they might be useful for reminding the pupils of what they have learned.
◆ Prepare some revision questions about each drug education lesson.

— USING THE ACTIVITY SHEET —

The focus of the activity is to consider various aspects of the series of drug education lessons by which to review and evaluate them.

Step 1   Display the sheets from Activity 1 and any others produced in the lessons. Hand each pupil their sheets from the rest of the lessons, as well as the one for this activity. Ask the pupils to look at the display and their sheets and to complete the new one.

Step 2   Place the four large sheets in different parts of the room. Organise a way for all the pupils to write their responses on each sheet, adding the same or similar comments close to one another.

Step 3   Split the class into pairs. Ask four pairs to look at one of the sheets each and to prepare a brief presentation on its contents. Ask the other pairs to prepare a revision question about something from the course, to which they know the answer.

Step 4   Alternate presentations about the review sheets with a few questions.

Extension Activities

◆ Ask the pupils to use the information sources they have gathered to attempt to deal with the elements that the class decided were omitted from the course. The final report should be written up and presented to the teacher.
◆ Using information they have gathered, ask the pupils to design their ideal series of drug education lessons.

Outcomes

◆ A review of the drug education lessons.
◆ Review, revision and presentation skills.

Absolutely spliffing!

1. Write your opinion of the drug education lessons in the drawings.

The best lessons.

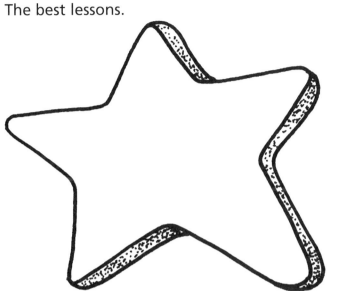

The most important thing you have learned.

What was missing?

How could it be improved?

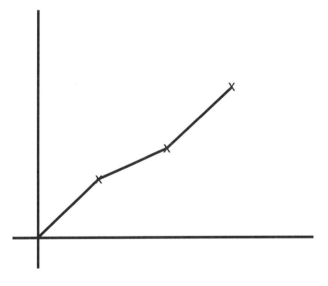

2. Write some revision questions for the drug education lessons, making sure that you know the answers.

_____

_____

_____

_____

Alcohol

Drug name	**Alcohol**.
Slang names	Booze, plonk, drink, bevvies, Dutch courage, six-pack, etc.
Brand names	Guinness, Claret, Southern Comfort, etc.
Description	Swallowed as a drink. Subject to licensing regulations. Strength varies from product to product, but must be shown on the labelling.
Group	Depressant.
Legal status	Possession and use legal from age 5. Purchase of beer, cider, perry (and wine in Scotland) permitted at age 14 in licensed restaurants to drink with a meal. Purchase from licensed premises (pub, off-licence) permitted from age 18. Sale to under 18s forbidden on these premises. Possession an offence on some trains and coaches to designated sporting events.
Effects short term	Absorbed into bloodstream after 5–10 minutes. Effects of one 'unit' (glass of wine, half pint of ordinary beer, single measure of spirits) last for approximately 1 hour. Small doses cause light-headedness, relaxation and reduced inhibition. Larger doses progressively impair judgement, balance and coordination, cause vomiting and severe reduction of mental and physical function and can lead to unconsciousness. Small people are affected more. Death from acute alcohol poisoning possible if dose is large enough. Low inhibition often contributes to violent or other criminal behaviour.
Effects long term	Obesity and physical damage to brain, liver and kidneys is only visible after substantial tolerance and dependence have developed. Also disruption of lifestyle and the aggravation of personal, social and financial problems. Foetal damage possible for heavy drinking, pregnant mothers.
Principal danger/ other implications	Any situation demanding control and judgement, such as driving or balance. Poisoning for small, unhabituated person. Heavy use often accompanied by poor diet. Possibility of dependence.

Akyl nitrites

Drug name	**Alkyl nitrites** (amyl nitrite, butyl nitrite, iso-butyl nitrite).
Slang names	Poppers, hard core, room freshener.
Brand names	Liquid Gold, Stud, Rush, KIX, Rock Hard, Locker Room.
Group	Stimulant.
Legal status	Legal. None is restricted under the Misuse of Drugs Act, though amyl nitrite is a medicine.
Description	A sweet-smelling, volatile, yellow liquid sold in small brown bottles from some sex shops, joke shops and clubs. Strong following in gay clubs.
Effects short term	A strong stimulant, usually inhaled from soaked material. A euphoric rush is almost immediate and lasts only a few minutes. Dizziness and light-headedness accompany dilated blood vessels and a rush of blood to the brain. Some users report enhanced sexual pleasure. Nausea, cold sweats, dermatitis and painful nasal passages are less frequently reported. Glaucoma can be aggravated. Unconsciousness is possible if the user is lying down and gets up too quickly. Excessive use can cause a serious reduction of oxygen in the blood, which can be fatal.
Effects long term	Tolerance develops after a few weeks of use. No reports of any dependence. No serious long-term consequences documented.
Principal danger/ other implications	People with heart trouble, anaemia or glaucoma should avoid nitrites. Excessive use is hazardous.

Amphetamines and anabolic steroids

Drug name	Amphetamines.
Slang names	Speed, whizz, uppers, Billy, sulphate.
Brand names	Dexedrine, Ritalin and milder drugs like Tenuate Dospan.
Group	Stimulant.
Description	Synthetic stimulants used to treat hyperactivity and chronic tendency to fall asleep. Milder varieties used to treat obesity. Most 'street' amphetamine sulphate (powder, pills) are unlawful.
Legal status	All amphetamines are prescription-only medicines. Most are also Class B. Prepared for injection, they are Class A. A few milder variants are Class C.
Effects short term	A similar effect to that of adrenaline on someone feeling stress in an emergency. Users feel more energetic and confident. Higher doses make users feel 'capable of anything' and stimulate creativity. Anxiety, irritability and restlessness may follow as the body's energy is used up. Effects last 3–4 hours. After they wear off, users feel tired and hungry. Full recovery can take 1–2 days. Frequent high doses can produce delirium, panic and a form of temporary paranoia known as amphetamine psychosis.
Effects long term	Tolerance develops, tempting users to increase the dose. This in turn makes delusions and paranoid feelings more likely. Prolonged, heavy use exaggerates the symptoms. Resultant lack of sleep and nourishment can be serious and raised blood pressure may damage the heart and circulation.
Principle danger/ other implications	Taking too little account of the body's need to replenish sleep and nourishment. Injection of any substance is hazardous unless carefully and hygienically conducted.

Drug name	Anabolic steroids.
Slang names	Steroids, 'roids.
Brand names	Dianabol, Stanozolol, Durabolin, etc.
Group	Stimulants.
Description	Hormones mostly derived from testosterone and used to treat anaemia, thrombosis and weakened muscles. Used non-medically to build up muscle bulk.
Legal status	Prescription-only medicines and Class C. Possession for personal use without prescription is not an offence.
Effects short term	Often used by athletes and bodybuilders in doses far greater than therapeutically recommended. Reports of steroid-induced aggression ('roid rage) are common, opinions differ about whether this is a result of the drugs. Also, no conclusive evidence about whether increased muscle strength derives from steroids or an aggressive outlook by determined improvers.
Effects long term	Side effects are difficult to replicate clinically because athletes' doses are often unethically high. Reports include: liver abnormalities, tumours, hypertension, stunted growth, low sperm counts, temporary psychiatric problems, psychological dependence, (rare) permanent enlargement of male breasts with some steroids, increased female sex drive and enlarged clitoris, permanent female growth of facial and body hair, deepening voice and decrease in breast size – which all may be passed to a foetus by a pregnant user. Sharing needles can pass infections.
Principal danger/ other implications	Considerable, and sometimes permanent, physical changes. No improvement in athletic strength or performance. Injection is always hazardous unless careful and hygienic.

Caffeine and cannabis

Drug name	Caffeine, found in coffee, tea, some soft drinks and chocolate.
Slang names	Cuppa, espresso, cappuccino, coke, etc.
Brand names	Nescafe, PG Tips, Pepsi-Cola, Pro-Plus, Herbal Booster.
Group	Stimulant.
Description	Caffeine is the ingredient in tea and coffee which enables its drinkers to 'get going' in the mornings and to 'keep going' after afternoon tea-break. It replaced cocaine in Coca-Cola in 1904.
Legal Status	Legal. In the UK, 70% of adults drink coffee and 86% drink tea. Pro-Plus tablets available without prescription from pharmacies.
Effects short term	Like all stimulants, caffeine stimulates the nervous system and makes the user feel more awake and alert, moderate doses reducing the chance of boredom and tiredness. Larger doses reduce coordination. Caffeine can increase heart rate and raise blood pressure. It is a diuretic. When effects wear off, the user may feel more tired. Excessive doses, for example 15 cups of instant coffee, may cause insomnia, muscle tremor, diarrhoea and vomiting. Possible progression to delirium.
Effects long term	A pattern of 7–10 cups of strong tea or coffee a day can cause chronic anxiety, irritability and headache. Chronic insomnia is possible. Regular users may feel tired and irritable if they miss a single usual intake, particularly in the early morning.
Principal danger/ other implications	Possible increased risk of stomach ulcers with heavy use and aggravation of existing ulcers.

Drug name	**Cannabis**, hashish, marijuana, leaves or derivatives from the cannabis Sativa plant.
Slang names	Pot, blow, draw, wacky backy, dope, puff, smoke, spliff, hash, skunk, ganja, grass, etc.
Group	Hallucinogen.
Description	Leaf or derived resin or oil, are typically mixed with tobacco and smoked. Leaf, ('herbal' cannabis or 'grass') may be smoked alone. Resin may be mixed in food and eaten.
Legal status	Class B. Hash oil may be Class A, as are all extracted active ingredients from the plant: 'cannabinoids'. Cannabis accounts for the majority of all drug offences.
Effects short term	Effects start a few minutes after smoking and may last an hour or more. Dependent largely on users' moods and expectations, most don't find much to enjoy at first and have to learn to 'steer' the experience. Relaxation and a heightened sense of colour, sound and taste, may follow, with a state of well-being. Short-term memory loss is commonly reported, as are giggling and hunger. Higher doses alter sense of time and other perceptual distortions and can cause confusion and distress.
Effects long term	No conclusive evidence of physical damage. Inhalation of smoke is likely to contribute to respiratory disorders (though quantities used are likely to be significantly smaller than tobacco and therefore the dangers are reduced). Chronic use may lead to apathy and poor general performance and can aggravate existing or latent mental illness.
Principal danger/ other implications	Use when not feeling 'in harmony' with self or surroundings. Driving while affected. Developing a frequent heavy pattern of use. Getting caught.

Cocaine

Drug name	Cocaine, 'crack'.
Slang names	Charlie, coke, snow, C (cocaine), rock, wash, stone, freebase (crack).
Brand names	None.
Group	Stimulants.
Description	Cocaine is a white powder (cocaine hydrochloride). It is usually sniffed up the nose ('snorted') or injected. Crack (raisin-sized crystals) is a freebase form of the same drug and is usually 'smoked' (heated and then vapour inhaled).
Legal status	Class A under the Misuse of Drugs Act. Rarely used medically (occasionally as anaesthetic for eye operations).
Effects short term	Cocaine is a strong nervous stimulant, making the user feel exhilarated and impressive and causing indifference to hunger, tiredness and pain. It can also cause anxiety and panic. Effects can last 20 minutes or more. With crack, the effects start earlier but are shorter lived. As with its cheaper rival, amphetamine, large or frequently repeated doses may cause extreme agitation, hallucinations and paranoia, which subside as the drug is eliminated from the body.
Effects long term	Tolerance and physiological dependence do not develop. Psychological dependence may be strong, particularly if smoked. Snorting can damage nasal membranes. Smoking can cause respiratory weakness. Regular users may be hyper-excitable, restless and nauseous and may find it hard to sleep. Temporary psychosis and chronic nervousness are possible until use is stopped.
Principal danger/ other implications	Injection of any substance is hazardous unless carefully and hygienically conducted. Euphoric feelings diminish if 'chased'. Emotional dependence may be hard to break. Heavy use is expensive.

Ecstasy

Drug name	Ecstasy: 3, 4, methylene-dioxymethamphetamine, known as 'MDMA'.
Slang names	E, XTC, Dennis the Menace, Love Doves, Disco Biscuits, etc.
Brand names	None.
Group	Stimulants; technically, ecstasy is a hallucinogenic amphetamine.
Description	Usually coloured pills or capsules, illicitly manufactured. Pills may have a motif moulded into them, such as a dove. Capsules may have different coloured ends, for instance red and black – Dennis the Menace.
Legal status	Class A under the Misuse of Drugs Act. No medical uses.
Effects short term	Strong stimulant. Early effects include tightening of the jaw, brief nausea, sweating and dry mouth, followed by feelings of alertness, euphoria, serenity and calmness and empathy towards those around. Full effects may take up to an hour to emerge. Deaths have occurred which are directly associated with ecstasy. Most symptoms seem to have been similar to acute heatstroke. Some users have had a heart attack or brain haemorrhage following high blood-pressure, due to the stimulant effect. Excessive intake of water has been noted in two or three deaths, made worse by ecstasy's capacity to reduce flow of water through the body.
Effects long term	Tolerance develops but not physical dependence. There is some evidence of liver damage among ecstasy users. No evidence of foetal damage, but women with history of genito-urinary tract infection should avoid this drug as should anyone with heart disease, high blood-pressure, glaucoma, epilepsy or poor mental or physical shape.
Principal danger/ other implications	Overheating and dehydration, due to combined effect of drug and sweating from exertion, such as dancing in an enclosed space with others. Long-term effects as yet unknown but seem to increase the chance of psychological problems.

Heroin

Drug name	**Heroin** and other opiates. Includes those refined from the opium poppy: codeine, morphine and synthetic opioids like pethidine, methadone. Also, painkillers such as Palfium, Temgesic and Distalgesic.
Slang names	H, horse, scag, junk, smack.
Brand names	Others include: Gee's Linctus, Codafen.
Group	Analgesics (painkillers).
Description	Heroin is a powder. Others appear in a variety of forms, apart from analgesic effects, for example cough suppressants and anti-diarrhoea agents.
Legal status	Class A under the Misuse of Drugs Act. Opium is the only controlled drug whose use is restricted, in addition to possession and supply. Prescriptions for all are permitted for medical use.
Effects short term	Powder can be sniffed ('snorted'), smoked ('chasing the dragon') or dissolved and injected. First tries can be unpleasant, causing nausea. Moderate doses depress nervous system and give euphoric feeling of warmth. Higher doses produce drowsy contentment and freedom from anxiety. Excessive doses induce coma. Overdose leading to death is possible, but not likely unless in combination with other drugs, or an unexpectedly pure sample. A high dose, after a gap sufficient to reduce tolerance, can constitute fatal overdose.
Effects long term	Tolerance and physical dependence develop. Withdrawal is similar to flu and less dangerous than withdrawal from alcohol.
Principal danger/ other implications	Addiction, criminal record and penalties associated with Class A drugs. Expensive. Progression to injecting to maximise the effects. Injection of any substance is hazardous unless carefully and hygienically conducted.

LSD and 'magic' mushrooms

Drug name	**LSD** – lysergic acid diethylamide.
Slang names	Acid, trips, tabs.
Brand names	None.
Group	Hallucinogens.
Description	A powerful drug, altering perceptual function. Derived from a fungus called ergot. Taken in tiny tablets or absorbed into small squares of paper, or gelatine sheets.
Legal status	Class A under the Misuse of Drugs Act.
Effects short term	Effects (known as a 'trip') begin within 30–60 minutes and typically last 12 hours. Senses are distorted and perceptions are so altered as to be hard to describe. Trips may be wonderful, uplifting and mystical, though some can be strange and terrible, particularly if the user is feeling negative or insecure. Sometimes trips vary between being good and bad within the same trip. True hallucinations are rarely reported. Concentration and, for example, driving ability are diminished. Trips cannot be stopped once they have started; a bad trip may run its course without improving.
Effects long term	No known physical dangers. Adverse psychological reactions have been reported but usually in people with some mental instability and after repeated uses. Tolerance develops rapidly but not physical dependence. Psychological dependence is rare.
Principal danger/ other implications	Psychotic episodes for users with latent (hidden) or embryonic (during the first stages) mental illness. Flashbacks, (trips re-lived briefly at later times) can be disorientating. Misjudging the time needed for a trip. Risking a trip when mood or demeanour is not favourable.

Drug name	**'Magic' (hallucinogenic) mushrooms.**
Slang names	'shrooms, mushies.
Brand names	None, most commonly gathered from the wild rather than purchased.
Group	Hallucinogens.
Description	Liberty Cap and Fly Agaric; naturally growing mushrooms with hallucinogenic properties. Up to 20–30 Liberty Caps may be needed for an extensive 'trip'.
Legal status	Possession or consumption is not restricted. Making 'a preparation or other product' by drying, cooking or infusing them renders them a Class A drug.
Effects short term	Similar to a mild LSD 'trip', often including euphoria and giggling. Shorter (4–9 hours) and quicker to start than LSD. Larger doses may cause stomach pains and vomiting. An anxious or stressed user may be more likely to have a 'bad' trip or even a psychotic episode. Negative effects are temporary.
Effects long term	As with LSD, tolerance develops. Much higher doses may be needed if the experience is to be repeated soon. This diminishes after a week or so. Little evidence of long-term harm, although psychological dependence is a possibility.
Principal danger/ other implications	Eating deadly poisonous varieties in error. (No deaths have been recorded so far.)

Solvents

Drug name	**Solvents** and other volatile and sniffable substances, such as butane gas, glue, toluene, acetone, fluorocarbons (propellants from aerosols), trichloroethane (cleaning fluid), petrol.
Group	Depressant.
Description	Gases and volatile substances giving off heavy vapour, inhaled from high pressure containers (fire extinguishers, lighter-fuel canisters, aerosols) or sniffed from plastic bags (glue, thinners), or soaked material to produce intoxication.
Legal status	The Intoxicating Substances Supply Act 1985, operates in England, Wales and Northern Ireland to restrict retailers from supplying solvents to anyone under the age of 18, if they have reason to believe the solvents will be used for the purposes of intoxication. Scotland has broadly similar arrangements under common law. Possession and use of solvents is not an offence, but in some areas by-laws allow police to take sniffers in public to 'a place of safety'. In Scotland, they can be taken into care.
Effects short term	Effects similar to alcohol, but shorter lived (typically 10–20 minutes). Vapour absorbed through lungs quickly reaches the brain. Reduced oxygen contributes to the effect. Coordination and balance are quickly impaired. Reduced inhibition leads to merriment and boisterousness. Deep inhalation can cause unconsciousness, though full recovery is usually quick. The toxic effects of, for example, lighter fuel have killed. Most deaths are due to the circumstances of sniffing (see 'principal dangers' below).
Effects long term	Long-term, heavy use of 10 years or so may lead to some brain damage. Similar patterns of sniffing aerosols, or cleaning fluids, have caused kidney and liver damage.
Principal danger/ other implications	There are five distinct hazards leading to deaths: sniffing from large plastic bag causing suffocation; loss of balance from tree, high window, canal bank and so on; freezing of airways resulting from squirting substance into the mouth, or nose, direct from a pressurised container; exertion after sniffing causing stress to the heart; vomiting following loss of consciousness.

Tobacco

Drug name	**Tobacco, containing nicotine.** Nicorette, Nicotinelle patches.
Group	Stimulant.
Description	Products containing dried leaves of tobacco plant. Usually burned and smoke inhaled. Can be chewed or sucked. Cannabis cigarettes ('joints', 'spliffs') usually contain tobacco as the main ingredient. Patches are sold to aid withdrawal from addiction.
Legal status	Legal to possess and smoke at any age. Supply is restricted to licence holders, who may not sell to under 16s, though purchase by under 16s is not restricted! Personal cultivation of tobacco plants is permitted. The use of tobacco is banned in many public places. Park keepers and police officers are still permitted to confiscate tobacco from under 16s.
Effects short term	Nicotine is absorbed rapidly by the lungs to reach the brain. Each inhalation has the same rapid, distinct effect, increasing heart rate and blood pressure and stimulating or arousing the user's nervous system, causing smokers to feel a reduction in stress and anxiety. First use often causes sick and dizzy feelings. Withdrawal causes restless irritability and depression, tempting further use.
Effects long term	Nicotine is addictive. The development of tolerance and dependence are marked and rapid. The more one smokes, the more likely are heart disease, blood clots, bronchitis, lung cancer, cancer of mouth and throat, to develop. Over 120 000 premature deaths occur each year in the UK from smoking-related disorders. If no irreversible damage has occurred, smokers may return to full health and life expectancy by stopping.
Principal danger/ other implications	Premature death. Passive smoking now considered a significant risk. Smaller, less mature babies born to smoking mothers. Diseases from oral contraceptives (for instance the female pill) are ten times more likely among smokers.

Tranquillizers

Drug name	**Tranquillizers** (term usually refers to minor tranquillizers, the benzodiazepines). Includes temazepam and diazepam.
Slang names	Tranx, moggies, mazzies.
Brand names	Valium, Ativan, Mogadon, etc.
Group	Depressant.
Description	The most commonly prescribed drugs in Britain, used to treat insomnia, anxiety and mental distress.
Legal status	Prescription-only medicines and in Class C. Possession of any tranquillizer except Temazepam without prescription is not itself an offence unless the drug has been illicitly produced.
Effects short term	Depress mental activity, cause drowsiness and forgetfulness, and impair driving skills, though only until habituation (a week or two of continuous use). Relief of anxiety and tension is pleasurable, but not for non-anxious users, hence the relative unpopularity among young people seeking excitement. High doses bring sleep, which can last into the following day. Overdose is rare, due to the number needed. However, if mixed with alcohol the fatal dose is lowered.
Effects long term	Tolerance and dependence, probably principally psychological in nature, develop within weeks. Medical effectiveness significantly reduced, or absent, within months. Withdrawal can cause great anxiety even when medical benefit is no longer gained from use. Withdrawal symptoms include insomnia, anxiety, irritability and vomiting. There are about 16 million prescriptions per year. Estimates suggest there are 1 million addicts among those given prescriptions.
Principal danger/ other implications	Mixing with alcohol; long-term dependence. Leaving within reach of small children. Observed regular intake may set example to young people.

ACTIVITY BANK: *Drugs* © Folens (copiable page)

The drug laws

There are two main sets of drug laws: the Medicines Act 1968 controls medical drugs; the Misuse of Drugs Act 1971 is intended to prevent the non-medical use of certain drugs. There are also laws concerning alcohol, tobacco and solvents.

Medicines Act 1968

This divides medical drugs into three groups:
- **Prescription-only medicines** can only be obtained with a doctor's prescription. It is illegal to give or sell them to anyone else.
- **Pharmacy medicines** don't need a prescription, but can only be bought from a pharmacy.
- **General sales list medicines** can be obtained without prescription from any shop.

The Misuse of Drugs Act 1971

	Class A	Class B	Class C
Drugs included:	opium; heroin, methadone; cocaine; crack; LSD, ecstasy, processed 'magic' mushrooms; any Class B drug prepared for injection	amphetamines; cannabis resin, 'herbal' cannabis and hash oil; barbiturates; codeine	mild amphetamines; tranquillizers, DF 118 (painkillers), (most) anabolic steroids
Maximum penalties for possession:	7 years and a fine	5 years and a fine	2 years and a fine
Maximum penalties for trafficking:	Life imprisonment and a fine	14 years and a fine	5 years and a fine

The above are the maximum penalties a Crown Court can impose. A magistrate is restricted to imposing a maximum of 6 months' imprisonment and a fine of £2000. It is important to realise that these maximum sentences will depend upon previous offences and other factors involved. They are not automatic. Minimum penalties are much less. Police have the power to caution and not prosecute in some situations.

Tobacco

It is illegal to sell cigarettes to under 16s.

Alcohol

It is an offence to give alcohol to a child under the age of five. At 14 a person can go into a bar, but not drink alcohol there. At 16 a person can drink beer, cider or perry (and wine in Scotland) served with a meal in an area set aside for dining. An 18 year-old can buy alcohol. It is an offence to be drunk in a public place, or to drive with a specific blood alcohol level in 100ml of blood. Local by-laws can prohibit drinking in public places.

Solvents

The Intoxicating Substances (Supply) Act 1985 makes it an offence to supply, or offer to supply, someone younger than 18 with solvents if it is known, or believed, that they are going to misuse them.

Glossary

ABUSE: Using drugs in a harmful way.

ADDICT: A drug user whose use causes them problems; 'problem drug user' is now preferred.

ADDICTION: A dependency that has serious detrimental effects on the drug user. As the term has negative connotations, 'dependence' is more accurate and neutral.

ADULTERATION: The dilution of a drug with other substances.

ANALGESIC: A painkiller.

BENZODIAZEPINES: The main group of tranquillizers.

BETA BLOCKER: A drug that calms people down by blocking the action of adrenaline.

COME DOWN: The experience as drug effects wears off.

CUT: To dilute a drug with other substances.

DESIGNER DRUG: A drug specifically synthesised to get round the law.

DEPENDENCE: The physical or psychological need to keep taking a drug.

DEPRESSANT: A drug that reduces the activity of the nervous system.

DETOXIFICATION: Withdrawing from the effects of a drug in a safe environment.

DRUG: A substance other than food that alters the body's structure or function.

EUPHORIA: Feeling exceptionally good.

FLASHBACK: The spontaneous recurrence of a hallucinogenic experience.

HABIT: Dependence on a drug.

HALLUCINATIONS: Experiences and sensations which are not real.

HALLUCINOGENS: Drugs that alter perceptual function.

HARD DRUGS: Drugs that people think are more dangerous than others. The term has no legal or medical validity and is therefore best avoided.

JOINT: A cannabis cigarette.

MAINLINE: To inject a drug into a vein.

MISUSE: Using drugs in a socially unacceptable way.

NARCOTIC: A drug such as heroin that induces drowsiness or insensibility. Often used in America to mean any illegal drug.

OPIATES: Drugs derived from the opium poppy.

OVERDOSE: An excessive, harmful amount of a drug.

PARAPHERNALIA: The equipment used for drug taking.

PROBLEM DRUG USE: Drug use that causes social, financial, psychological, physical, or legal problems for the user.

RECREATIONAL DRUG USE: The use of drugs for pleasure or leisure.

ROACH: The cardboard tip put into the end of a cannabis 'joint'.

SCORE: To buy drugs.

SEDATIVE: A depressant drug that reduces anxiety and induces calmness or sleep.

SHOOT UP: To inject drugs.

SMART DRUGS: Drugs that are supposed to increase mental performance.

SOFT DRUGS: The drugs that people think are less dangerous than others. The term has no legal or medical validity and is therefore best avoided.

SPLIFF: A cannabis cigarette.

STIMULANT: A drug that stimulates the nervous system.

STONED: Under the influence of drugs, usually cannabis.

TOLERANCE: A decreased response to a drug such that more is needed to produce an effect.

VOLATILE SUBSTANCES: A term used to cover all those substances that are sniffed.

WITHDRAWAL: The physical and psychological effects experienced on stopping taking a drug.

Useful addresses and resources

Institute for the Study of Drug Dependence
(ISDD)
32 Loman Street
London
SE1 OEE

Telephone: 0207 928 1211
Fax: 0207 928 1771
email: services@isdd.co.uk
website: http://www.isdd.co.uk

ISDD offers comprehensive, objective, current and accurate information in its publications, library service and website.

One of its publications, *Drug Abuse Briefing*, aquaints the general reader with the basic facts about drugs (both legal and illegal) used for non-medical purposes in the UK. An essential reference book for all teachers concerned with drug education.

Health Education Authority
Trevelyan House
30 Great Peter Street
London
SW1P 2HW

Telephone: 0207 222 5300
Fax: 0207 413 8900
Website: http://www.hea.org.uk

HEA offers a range of information and publications about health issues, including drugs. Its website has links to a variety of others relevant to drugs education.

The National Drugs Helpline offers free and confidential advice about drugs all day, every day, and can refer you on to local drugs services. Telephone: 0800 77 66 00

Release is a confidential helpline offering advice on drug use and legal issues. Telephone: 0207 603 8654

The following publications are available free of charge to support school drug education:

from the DfEE orderline (0845 602226):

Drug Education: Curriculum guidance for schools (SCAA/DfEE, 1995)

Protecting Young People: Good practice in drug education (DfEE, 1998)

The Right Choice: Guidance on selecting drug education materials for schools (SCODA, 1998)

The Right Approach: Quality standards in drug education (SCODA, 1999)

The Right Responses: Managing and making policy for drug-related incidents in school (SCODA, 1999)

from the Drug Campaign Information Service (DCIS – 01304 614731):

Drugs: the facts (for 11–14-year-olds)

The score: facts about drugs (for 14–16-year-olds)

D-mag (for 16–25-year-olds)

A Parent's Guide to Drugs and Alcohol

D-Code – a multimedia CD ROM about drugs for 13–19-year-olds

Skills matrix

ACTIVITY/ SKILL	1	2	3	4	5	6	7	8	9	10	11	12	13	14	15	16	17	18	19
Analysing/Interpreting								●					●						
Asserting		●							●	●		●		●	●		●		
Awareness	●	●	●	●	●	●	●	●	●	●	●	●	●	●	●	●	●	●	●
Collating	●						●	●					●	●				●	●
Communicating	●	●	●	●	●	●	●	●	●	●	●	●	●	●	●	●	●	●	●
Comparing	●	●		●			●	●	●	●				●			●	●	
Cooperating	●	●	●	●	●	●	●	●	●	●	●	●	●	●	●	●	●	●	●
Debating and discussing	●	●		●	●				●	●		●	●		●	●	●		
Decision making			●						●			●							
Empathising				●	●							●		●		●	●	●	
Evaluating			●		●				●	●	●	●	●				●		●
Expressing (e.g. of beliefs, ideas and opinions)	●	●	●	●	●	●	●	●	●	●	●	●	●	●	●	●	●	●	●
ICT	●					●			●				●						
Identity and self-esteem			●	●						●	●	●	●	●	●			●	
Imagining			●	●			●				●	●		●	●			●	
Investigating	●	●	●	●		●	●		●			●				●			
Knowledge	●	●	●	●	●	●	●	●	●	●	●	●	●	●	●	●	●	●	●
Listening	●	●	●	●	●	●	●	●	●	●	●	●	●	●	●	●	●	●	●
Negotiating		●												●					
Perceiving					●					●		●		●	●	●	●	●	
Presenting						●				●				●	●	●		●	●	●
Prioritising	●		●			●					●								
Problem solving											●						●		
Respect						●								●	●	●		●	
Responsibility										●				●	●				●
Understanding	●	●	●	●	●	●	●	●	●	●	●	●	●	●	●	●	●	●	●